Knowledge
Father To Son

By

Walter Mosely, Jr.

Walter Mosely, Jr.

ISBN 10:0983558604
ISBN-13:978-0-9835586-0-6:

DEDICATION

I lovingly dedicate this project to Jessica Marie Mosely also known as "Jessie Mae" and even deeper still Momma. For having the courage and insight at such a young age to know that the man she would give her all to would have such an impact on our household, our family, and the city of Port Arthur, Texas. Your courage has given all of us wings and now you are the wind beneath them. With all my love,

"Bozo"

Mr. and Mrs. Walter and Jessica Mosely, Sr.

CONTENTS

Acknowledgments   vi

Introduction   2

Chapters

1   Truth Equals Action   8

2   With Freedom Comes Responsibility   16

3   Listen Son, Just Listen   26

4   No Matter Where You Go, There You Are!   34

5   You Hear My Voice, Right?   42

6   Responsibility Is A Heavy Responsibility   56

7   Mind Your Front Row, Son   62

8   All Money Ain't Good Money   74

9   Check Your Lost And Found   86

10   Remember To Stay In Your Lane   94

    About The Author   102

ACKNOWLEDGEMENTS

First and foremost I would like to thank God for his many blessings. It is through him that all things are possible.

To Mellernea Mosely my amazingly gorgeous wife. Thank you for always believing in me and for allowing me to be your "Super Man."

To James and Carolyn Campbell. Thank you for, the continued mental stimulation.

To Nakia Cole. Thank you for the photos and your friendship.

To Deborah "Minnie" Harris. Thank you for all the editing and being a great example. Thank you Big Sis'.

To my Son Joshua Walter Mosely. Thank you for being the reason and giving me the inspiration to take on this project.

Finally to all who has contributed in one way or another for helping me make this book come to reality, many thanks.

Walter Mosely, Sr.

Introduction

On the advice of friends and other authors I was told that it was a good idea to allow as many people to read my manuscript as possible and to get their most honest and opinionated advice. After getting back a few of these responses—keep in mind this is before I actually finished the book—I found that 98 percent of the people I trusted to read it asked me the same question: "What prompted you to write this book at this time?" Were they asking what made me wait till I was 48 years old to write my very first book? Or were they asking what stimulated me to write about this particular subject? Or maybe they were asking what made me think I was smart enough to even write a book? Eventually I answered their loaded question.

I have always felt that my father was an amazing man even while I was growing up and saw him interact with others on a daily basis. I have often felt blessed that I grew up with a man who enjoyed answering my many annoying questions and continued to give me the wisdom that I would need for the rest of my life in many daily bite-sized portions.

My father gave his all to my day-to-day experiences and took the let-downs that I constantly gave him in stride and came back the next day fully loaded to give me even more love, strength, and understanding than before. Unfortunately, my father passed in May 1992 which represents the only regret that I own in my life: that my father did not live long enough to see my son, his only Mosely grandson.

My son Joshua was born in November the same year my father passed. I wish my son could have known this great man. He definitely hears the stories from my siblings and cousins but I would have liked him to have felt the warmth that was my father himself. In the years following my father's death I did all I could to hold fast to my father's teachings but the world has a way of making that straight-and-narrow difficult. Still, his wisdom found a way to guide me through the years, keeping me out of heavy trouble and keeping me going through the hard times.

I can still hear in the back of my mind some of my friends through the years asking me, "Man where do you get those down-home-country sayings from?" So the wisdom that was taught to me has always been there and on many occasions throughout my life I have relied on that old school wisdom to sustain my life's journey. But to write about them and what they meant to me was something that I could not even fathom, until now.

Just let me say this: for the last three-and-a-half to four years my now eighteen-year-old son has been coming home from high school with all sorts of questions. Questions about girls, life, drugs, money and for certain sex; and let me tell you, the answers are not always easy. In fact, for the most part, they were downright scary and hard to answer. The information that I am downloading into this young mind will eventually mold him into the young man and finally the grown man he will soon become. So the answers will have to be well thought out and meaningful enough so that he can rely on them for the long term and not just a quick fix. I need my son to get these lessons right the first time because this life is not very good at giving second chances and on those occasions when he does not get it just right I need him to be able to find his way back to the lessons that got him to that point in the first place—lessons he can use every day of his life. But today's generation has a language all of its own. They see Snoop Dog, Jay-Z, and Fifty Cent as the mark of success that they want to hit. They see the pants sagging halfway down their ass, the disrespect and mistreatment of women and material excess as the "cool" thing to do. So how do you meld wisdom, values, and common sense into a digestible easy to understand and memorable answer to some of life's most difficult questions and then feed this answer to a hungry mind waiting to absorb and execute anything you say for now and forevermore?

Well for me, first I pray, and then I think way back about how I was raised and the amazing job my father did answering my difficult questions. You see, my father has always been able to know what to say to make sure that I got the exact meaning of the answer that he gave me for any question that I asked. And usually it was done with some sort of old-timey saying or aphorism that on the surface was funny and had only a vague correlation to the question but after explanation was revealed to be spot-on accurate for the question that was asked. In short, my father had a saying for everything.   I wrote this book to save my son and I wrote this book to honor my father and I wrote this book to feed hope and wisdom to all that read it, and if you smile and giggle at some of the stories then that's okay, too. Please enjoy.

NOTES

Getting Sworn In For His Third Term

Chapter 1

Truth Equals Action

$\mathcal{M}_y$ father was a firm believer in the truth. He felt that the truth was so powerful that once you heard it you would have to do something about it. He felt that an action would have to occur because the "TRUTH" just would not allow you to sit still and do nothing. In my junior high school years, the truth hit my father so hard that we almost lost everything because he had to do something about it. My father was a self-employed real estate and insurance agent in a little town called Port Arthur, Texas. For a man who received his high school diploma on a ship from a correspondence course while sailing the waters as a seaman, he did quite well for himself and his family, especially considering the hard upbringing he'd had.

As the baby of nine children and seemingly the most responsible of them all, my father took care of his own seven kids, his mother until her death, and the kids of some of his siblings until they could take care of themselves. Despite his many responsibilities, in 1976 my father noticed that the west side of town where the black community was located had always been represented by a white council member who never seemed to have his constituents' best interests at heart. My father also noticed that the east side of town which was all white was always getting something new.

There were new parks, street curbs and gutters, cut and weeded grass, and trimmed trees on a regular basis on the east side. The even funnier thing about it was that the city councilman that represented the white people clear on the other side of town was the same councilman that represented the black people on our side of town.

About this same time, I was in the eighth grade and because we moved from the west side of town to what we called "the country," I now lived in an area that meant I had to go to Thomas Edison, a white junior high school. It was a weird transition for me to sit, talk, and eat next to white people every day. I mean, I had seen white people before and had some dealings with them, especially when I used to ride with my daddy while he was doing business, but that was just every now and then.

You have to understand that until I started junior high school, my everyday world was filled with blackness. My teachers were black, my fellow students were black, and the stores, car repair shops, cleaners, and flower shops, the barbeque restaurants, chicken shacks, car washes, fruit stands, gas stations, jewelry stores, clothing stores, and churches were all owned or operated by black people.

Not only that, but all these people that I saw in these places were people that I knew and knew very well. They were pillars of our community. These were strong, upstanding black people that you counted on because they knew you and your whole family. It was a good feeling to hear any of these people ask, "How are you doing today?" because you knew that they were genuinely concerned about the answer you gave back. I really miss those days. Sometimes I feel that integration was the worst thing that could have happened to black people. It took us away from us.

After many late nights and long evenings down at City Hall attending meetings and looking over charts and drawings of the city's voting districts and the city's voting history, my father saw that for the last forty years the people in power were trying to stay in power by what they call "Gerrymandering" the voting districts. You see, every so many years the mayor and the city council members would get together and re-draw the entire city's voting districts so that the white vote would always dilute the black vote and continue to keep the powers that be in power.

I remember many days and evenings coming home from school seeing rickety aluminum easels holding up faint white and blue-edged redistricting posters that my father had on display in the formal living and dining room of our house. Daily he would have two or three people over so he could explain to them (and to anyone else who would listen) how the mayor and city council members were basically stealing and rigging the election process to maintain power of "our tax dollars." Everyone that heard his message would "Ooh" and "Ahh" and say, "That's a damn shame!" They could not believe that this was happening to them. But then they would leave the house with no plans to contribute to the effort or to give money to help do something about it.

Speaking of money, the powers that be began slowing down my father's income as a way of trying to control him and make him shut up. You see, when you sell a house it takes a long time to get paid, at least thirty days. Appraisals take time, mortgage companies take time, closings take time, title searches take time, and these things can tie up your money. For some reason, they were taking longer than usual—and not just one or two deals but every deal.

To top that off, I was getting into arguments and fights with the white kids as well as the black kids at school because they would say my dad was a troublemaker and that he thought he was better than them and that all he wanted to do was get on the news or see his picture in the newspaper.

In the meantime, between the City Hall meetings and the living room presentations I did not get to spend much time with my father. He was deep into the truth but all the truth did for me was distance me from my father and give me daily grief at school. I sat my father down and asked him to please let this go. I told him that we were not spending much time together, that people all over town were mad at him, that the money situation was getting worse, and that it looked like everyone he told didn't care anyway. He put his hand on my shoulder as a way of saying, "brace yourself" as he always did when something heavy was about to be laid on me.

He said, "Son, the truth is like accidently sitting on a thumb tack; it makes you jump up and do something about it. Everyone has his own truth to fight for, and this one is mine. When you find yours, you will have to give it action too because it is yours. But don't give up, Son, because the truth will always win. Your truth will create action."

After that my father went through the whole process with me. He showed me over the years how the voting lines had been moved around and how adjacent cities had been annexed or incorporated to dilute the black vote. Then he showed me the money that was coming in from the taxes and what was being done with that money. Then he drove me to both sides of town to show me what the disparity between black neighborhoods and white neighborhoods looked like and how the differences were so extreme.

Then he said, "Now when you go back to school and the kids razz you with name-calling and talking about what your father is doing, you hit them with the truth and see what happens then." The next day I could not wait to go to school. I had ammunition now and I let everyone have it with both barrels. By the end of the week, my government teacher had asked me to give a presentation on Gerrymandering. I'd come off like a hero.

That's the action that I gave to my truth. Here is what my father did with his truth: he sued the city of Port Arthur for unfair re-districting and wrongful gerrymandering of the city's districts. The case went all the way to the Justice Department of the United States in Washington, D.C. And he won. He also created a fairer redistricting plan called single-member districts that is still used in the city of Port Arthur today.

My father did not win money or fame; he just won the right for the people of the city of Port Arthur to have fair and just elections. Oh, and by the way, by the urging of the people, he ran for a city councilman seat and won that, too…three terms.

My Good Best Friend Mark Edward Taylor

Chapter 2

With Freedom Comes Responsibility

$\mathcal{B}$etween the ages of zero and nine years old my best good friend in the whole wide world was Mark Edward Taylor. Mark lived about half a block away from me. In fact, he lived so close to me that we used to look at each other through the windows of our houses while we talked to each other on the phone. So we saw and played together each and every day. Our birthdays were only nine days apart: Mark's was September 20th and mine was September 29th. So, quite naturally, we celebrated a lot of our birthdays together, and they were always fun.

Mrs. Elnora, Mark's mother, worked as a cook at a hotel restaurant called the Driftwood Inn, and Mark stayed with us during the day until she got off work. Then Mark would walk across the street when he saw his mother's car in the driveway. Mark was brought up in a house with three older brothers and Mrs. Elnora. Back in the day we called our elders by their first names preceded by *Mr.* or *Mrs.* as a sign of respect and as a show of love because we were so much like family back then.

But anyway, Mark's brothers' ages coincided with the ages of my siblings so that also made us close. Glen, Mark's oldest brother, was about the same age as my oldest sister, Belinda; Christopher or "Buster" was about the same age as my sister Deborah and my brother Steven. Robert was the same age as my brother Dwight, and they were close friends also. But Mark and I were practically twins. Well, I say twins because we spent so much time growing up together, but we certainly did not look anything alike. Mark and his brother Robert were very big and heavy "fellas," so much so that they earned their nicknames: "Big Meat" for Robert and "Little Meat" for Mark since he was Robert's little brother. Mark was a cute kid though; he was brown-skinned with curly, wavy hair. He had this big fat round face and big fat arms and legs. He looked like a little Samoan or Hawaiian. But he was always my *best*, good friend. Whenever people wanted to jump Mark or me, they knew they would have to take us both on. That was something you just did not want to do because that was a fight to the finish, and everyone knew it.

One year for my birthday, I had gotten a brand new Schwinn bicycle which was great for Mark and me because now we had the freedom of transportation. You see, Mark and I would always get left behind when the big kids took off on their bicycles and came back with all types of stories about what they had done and the things they had seen. But not anymore. We now had the freedom to go wherever and whenever we wanted, just like them. *In fact, why shouldn't we ride the bicycle to school? Yeah!*

Up until that day my father had driven Mark and me to Carver Elementary School and picked us up afterwards to take us home which was a bit embarrassing. Mark and I complained that all the other kids were calling us "sissies" and "little girls" because they were walking or riding their bikes to and from school. So Mark and I wanted to do the same.

My father asked Mark and me if we could handle that much freedom and the responsibility that went with it, like getting to school on time and coming straight home afterwards every day. We said that we could, and we did—for about a month.

You see, when my father drove us to and from school in the car, the distance seemed so short and the ride so quick and smooth. He would drop us real close to the gate of the school so that all we had to do was walk through the gate and onto the sidewalk and our classes were right there. Well, let me tell you something—those eighteen blocks became agony Mark and me.

I had to ride on the handlebars of the bicycle and that got uncomfortable real fast because Mark was not easy on the bumps. Mark had to pump the bicycle with me on the handle bars up all those hills to get to school. When we finally did make it to school we had to park the bicycle in the bicycle rack on the other side of the school by the gymnasium, chain it, lock it, and then run like hell to make it to class on time. Oh, and because it took more time to get to school now, we had to go to bed earlier the night before so we could get up earlier the morning of school to take that horrid ride again.

Needless to say I was looking for a way out of that misery. It turned out I didn't like the freedom I'd gotten from being able to come and go as I pleased nor did I like the responsibility that came with it, like going to school or going to the store every time somebody wanted something. It was just too much! One morning when Mark and I were taking the path to school, I looked up and saw the old Hempstead place. This was a house that had been vacant for as long as I could remember. It sat right next to a vacant lot where we played football sometimes.

I had a thought: "What if we went in there for just a minute or two to give my butt a rest, then take off again for school?" Mark was up for it because we had just finished climbing one hill and we had two more to go before we made it to school.

So we stopped at the house and looked around and found a back window that had been broken out some time ago and went on in.

The inside of the house looked like no one had ever moved out. There were beds, living room furniture, curtains, pots and pans, everything you could think of. If the place had had electricity and running water, we could have lived there. We had a fine old time in the old Hempstead house. In fact, so much fun that we got tired and thought we would lie down for a while and take a nap and then go to school late. I was sure we could make up some sort of excuse. When we woke up we did not know what time it was, but we heard the afternoon whistle blow from the refinery signaling 3:30 pm—the end of the work day.

Mark and I heard the whistle at the same time everyday as we rode the bicycle home from school. Then that day I thought, "Hey we could do this anytime we are tired or don't feel like going to school." It was perfect. We would just hold up there until we heard the afternoon whistle and then we could go home and no one would ever know."

After about the fourth or fifth time of our skipping school we had gotten it down to a "T." We would play around for a couple of hours or so then go to sleep and when we woke up, we would listen for the whistle to blow and go home like everything was a-okay. Perfect, right?

Except, for this one time when we decided to deviate from the plan. Instead of playing for a couple of hours or so then taking a nap, we decided to take a nap first then wake up and play and wait for the afternoon whistle. Same plan, same formula, but with a little twist. What could go wrong? We found out: everything. The formula that had been working always put us waking up around 1:30 or 2:00 and then the afternoon whistle would blow at 2:45 or 3:00—right about the time we would be riding our bicycle home. But because this time we took a nap first and then got up and played for an hour or so that whistle that we now heard was the noon-time lunch whistle, *not* the afternoon go-home whistle.

Mark and I strutted proudly into the house and announced, "We're hungry; can we eat now?" like we always did when we came home from school. But this time, Mom asked a peculiar question.

She said, "Uh, what are you two doing home so early?" At that moment I felt a very frosty chill down my spine, and I stuttered as I tried to explain my presence at high noon instead of my normal time.

"What you mean, Momma? The, the whi, whi, whistle blew and we're home now like every day."

She looked at the clock on the wall in the kitchen and said, "Boy that's the refinery's lunch time whistle. You been skipping school! Bring your little narrow ass here. I'm gonna'…" Needless to say, Mark got it, too.

I kind of felt sorry for Mark because not only would he get a lick or two from my mother and father, but he had to go home and get it from Mrs. Elnora, too, and Mrs. Elnora *didn't play*. She had four boys and no husband; she had to be harder than most. When my father made it home and after he got deep into my ass with that belt, he sat me down as he always did after some form of punishment and talked to me about how I'd let him down with the way I had set aside my responsibilities of school and how I had abused my new-found freedom.

He said, "As you get older, Son, you will acquire more and more freedom. You'll have more freedom to do what you want with your time, more freedom to do what you want with your money, and more freedom to express your thoughts. It is very important that you learn how to use your freedom to handle your responsibilities because one cannot exist without the other. As you get more freedom, you will automatically acquire more responsibilities. It is the person who evenly spreads them out or balances them so that one does not cancel out the other that creates the *person* that one is destined to be. Real freedom always comes with responsibility."

NOTES

\

My Son and I

Chapter 3

Listen Son, Just Listen

My father used to do some accounting work for Moody Harris Funeral Home. But because my father was so well known in the city as a fair and honest man, many came to talk to him to consult about their pre-need funeral arrangements. So he ended up taking a part-time job as a burial counselor for the funeral home. Of course, I was with him as much as possible, even there. Most people would be afraid to run around a funeral home, but not me.

My father used to tell me, "The dead cannot hurt you, Son, only the living." Plus I knew that if my father was near there was nothing bad that could happen to me, so I ran around the parlor knocking over caskets, spilling urns, and just generally causing the havoc I was known to create.

Around that time I had my first elementary school crush on a girl by the name of Terri Green. I don't really remember what she looked like, but in my mind she was beau-ti-ful. But everyone else, including my sisters, declared she was "ugly as hell." I also remember that I was in constant competition for her affections with an arch-rival of mine who lived across the street from me named John Levell.

We both had very light complexions and curly hair. I wore my hair short but John wore his long. I remember he had freckles and big buck teeth in the front. I don't know what Terri or any other girl saw in him; he looked down right goofy to me. Anyway, I remember how I first met Terri.

I had been with my father a couple of years before when my father had sold Terri's father and mother an insurance policy. I particularly remember my father nudging Mr. Green to get a policy that cost a couple of dollars more per month but with coverage that was almost doubled. My father promised that he would be happy with it, and so Mr. Green agreed.

Well a few years later Terri's mother was killed in a car accident and her father came to Moody Harris Funeral Home to make arrangements for the funeral. When he saw that my father was going to be the person taking care of his wife's funeral arrangements he hugged my father and started crying. My father did not say a word—he just waited for Mr. Green to finish sobbing and they both sat and began talking.

Mr. Green mentioned that he was very grateful for the sound insurance advice and that he was happy that my father had steered him in the other policy's direction. He mentioned that the policy that he'd gotten from my father would go much further in providing for his family's security. After they talked a little more about the insurance they switched to the subject of the funeral arrangements. I noticed that Mr. Green got very silent as did my father. What was so weird to me was that my father barely said a word at all and that Terri's father did not speak much either. Once or twice I noticed my dad would walk around his desk and just put his hand on Mr. Green's shoulder.

Mr. Green would cry a little bit and stop then my father would go back around the desk, and they would continue to hammer out the arrangements. Terri's father hugged and cried on my father's shoulder quite a bit that night but still my father barely spoke a word.

When Terri saw her father crying she began to cry. I felt compelled to do something. I wanted to help her like my dad had helped her father, but I really did not know what to do. Somewhere something inside of me said I had to do something.

So I started out by saying, "It's okay, everything will be alright," because that's what I had heard everyone else say at other funerals.

But, Terri snapped back. "No, it won't be alright. My mommy's dead, and she ain't ever coming back. Tell me how it will be alright?"

I was stunned. It had seemed to calm the other people down but it did nothing for Terri except make her sadder than she was before she came in. I tried to think of something good to say but nothing was coming out. Then I thought, what did the older folks say at the funerals I had been seeing? Then, it hit me.

I said, "Well at least she is with Jesus now and that's a good thing."

Terri began to cry harder and then she shouted, "I don't want her to be with Jesus. I want her to be here with me right now!"

I was completely lost then, and Terri was crying uncontrollably. So I tried to hug her to comfort her like other folks did, but she began to fight me off. I was done; I ran and hid in the back office where they kept all the show coffins, and I did not come out until my father came to look for me.

When my father found me all huddled up in a corner he asked me what had happened. So I ran down the whole story for him. I told him how I had just been trying to comfort Terri like I had seen so many other people do and how she'd just flipped out on me. I asked my father if she and Mr. Green were still there, and my father told me that they had left and that Terri was still very upset. I swore to my father that I hadn't done or said anything to hurt her intentionally and that I would apologize whenever I had the chance to see her again.

He assured me that he understood, and he knew that in my heart I had only been trying to help. Then I asked my father how had he done it, how had he gotten Mr. Green to keep calm and go through what had to be one of the most difficult moments of a man's life—planning a funeral for his wife with his daughter sitting close by? How did he do that with barely saying a word to him?

My father put his hand on my shoulder and said. "Son, the most basic and powerful way to connect to another human being is to listen, just listen. Perhaps the most important thing we can ever give each other is our attention. A loving silence often has far more power to heal and to connect than the most well-intentioned words."

The next day I asked my father to take me over to Terri and Mr. Green's house so that I could apologize to Terri for upsetting her.

For about thirty minutes I sat on the front porch steps with Terri Green—barely a word was spoken but with her hand in mine I felt like we were reading the dictionary to each other.

Eat your heart out John Levell…

NOTES

My Ten-Year-Old Birthday Party

Chapter 4

No Matter Where You Go, There You Are!

$\mathcal{I}$f you were to ask any of my family members or friends to describe me or to explain to you the person that I am, I can promise you that you would get the exact answer from each and every one of them. This I owe to my father and what he told me when I didn't know who I was or who to be.

My father was a self-employed realtor and insurance agent for forty years. And within those forty years of doing that business he dealt with all types of people: rich, poor, black, white, Asian, Hispanic. He dealt with people buying residential property, commercial property, people with great credit, and people with poor or no credit at all. During all that time I saw the same smile, handshake, and personality with each encounter. I never really thought much about it until my father brought it to my attention one day.

On September 29, 1972, I was nine going on ten years old. That's right; it was my birthday and my parents were throwing me a birthday party. Now this was a particularly rough time in my life because not too long before this particular birthday, my entire family had picked up and moved to the other side of town called El Vista, or as everyone else called it "the country." Where we used to live was always called "in town." I never saw anything wrong with where we'd lived in town. In fact, I kind of wished we had stayed in the old house on 1048 Roosevelt Street.

Nowhere else in my life have I ever felt quite like I was at home. I have often wondered what my life would have been like had we not moved from that little patch of land on the west side of town. My father had worked hard at his business and saved up enough money to buy a piece of land out there in the country, and he was very proud of it too. I remember how twice a month or so Momma and Daddy used to gather all of us and the lawn mower into the station wagon, and Daddy would get out there with a power mower and walk every inch of the property cutting that grass with a smile on his face. I guess it was the sense of ownership and the promise of a brighter future for his family that kept that smile on his face while cutting that big yard on those long hot summer days in Texas. I can remember thinking that if the grass was going to grow that high every two weeks, I did not want to move out there because sooner or later my older brothers would be gone from the house, and Daddy was going to make me cut it by myself.

Daddy used to say, "I'm going to build a house out here big enough for all of us to live comfortably, and me and your momma will be happy with all this peace and quiet."

"Yeah, quiet for you watching me cutting that damn yard," I thought. But eventually it happened. My mother and father actually drew up their own plans for our house in the country and had it built to his own personal specifications. It was beautiful and huge.

The house had four bedrooms with three-and-a-half bathrooms, a formal dining room with a sunken formal living room (which I had never seen before), a den with a huge kitchen, a foyer, a two-car garage, a totally separate laundry room with its own bathroom, and my daddy's office—altogether about 3,800 square feet. It was a beautiful home, and we were very happy there.

But what made things so difficult for me was that I left my whole world there on 1048 Roosevelt on the west side of town: my best good friend Mark Taylor, Jason Dixon, Tyra Dorsey, her sister Debra, their cousin Sarah, and Doris, Mark's cousin. This was our gang and I was the leader of the gang. I was the one everyone looked to for answers, the one to say what the agenda was for the day. If we had problems I was the one to figure them out. If there were issues or fights within the gang I was the one who settled them. I was the smart guy. This was my identity, my reality for the first nine years of my life. The alleys in which we played marbles, the backyards in which we raided plum trees, the mailbox where we met to fight on the way home, the baseball field where I received cuts and scratches—all these were now on the other side of town. Now, I had to forge a new identity. There were new faces, new personalities, and new issues I now had to confront. The people I was around now liked to swim in swimming holes naked. They liked hunting with BB guns, fishing with sticks, and digging up worms for the bait. I'd never done those things before.

I'd become a follower and not the leader. I had to take orders from someone else. I was now the dumbest kid on the block because I had to be taught everything. And they treated me funny like I was some rich spoiled kid because my father had built this big brand new house.

"He thinks he's rich," they used to say. I found myself fighting and defending myself quite a lot those days. So to cut down the confusion and to just fit in, I became another person. I became one of them to make it easier to go with the flow. And I dreaded it every single day.

But, as I was saying, it was my birthday and my birthday party and I was anxious about the fact that I honestly did not know who I should be because attending my birthday party would be kids from both sides of the tracks, so to speak. There would be my old friends from "in town" who knew me as a leader, the smart, funny kid who was always in the center of things and my new friends with whom I had to pretend not to know so much or be a leader or voice my opinions about the things I wanted and did not want to do. This was scary.

I tried to solve the whole situation by telling my father I did not want the party and to cancel it. But after much discussion my father finally got it out of me that I was afraid to be ME. Then my father gently laid his hand on my shoulder and explained to me that I would never know true happiness or achieve any personal satisfaction or fulfillment if I first did not know who I was.

His words were, "How will you know if you are happy if you do not know who you are? If you are a certain way on one side of town and then become a different way on the other side of town, then who are you? You will have to find a way to be you no matter what the situation or people you face so that no matter where you go, there YOU are."

Needless to say, I am the same kid that I was at ten years old from 1048 Roosevelt Street and I always will be.

NOTES

Deborah   Belinda   Vanessa   Victoria

Dwight   Steven   Walter, Jr.

The Mosely Siblings, 1991

Chapter 5

You Hear My Voice, Right?

𝔗o some, I'm sure that growing up in a house with seven kids would just be too many people under one roof. But in the neighborhood I grew up in, we were the rule not the exception. Right across the street from our house was the Wilson family—they had ten kids, half a block up the street from them was the Cunningham family—they had eleven kids, and then around the corner from us were the Johnsons who not only had thirteen kids but also had the nerve to start each of their kids names off with the letter "A." Now ain't that special? I know this because my oldest brother, Steven, married Angela Johnson. They had one daughter together and named her Tanya, but there will be more about them later.

The families in my neighborhood averaged about five kids per family so, needless to say, on a sunny day we had a pretty busy block. In my neighborhood there was a sense of family, a sense of belonging to something larger than yourself, and you felt the cohesion of that. Looking out for the kids in your neighborhood was like looking out for one of your own sisters or brothers. You felt your worth, your value; it gave you a defined meaning in the community because you always knew exactly who you were, and because of this community you had a good sense of what you might become.

It was everyone's responsibility on the block to raise you to your best potential. If someone fell by the wayside you felt like you all had a hand in that failure. You knew everybody and everybody knew you—if not by sight then for sure by your last name or the family you came from. I can remember doing something wrong around the neighborhood and catching a whipping by the nearest adult.

The adults always said, "You know your parents raised you better than that," and you knew it was the truth. Then they would call your parents and let them know what had happened and you would catch another whipping when you got home. But the second whipping you caught at home was not for what you did wrong at the neighbor's house but for embarrassing the family name "outside of the home." And this is where you always heard the lesson of, "You hear my voice, right?"

There was some good and a lot of bad for me growing up the last child or the baby of a large family. Because of the six others that came before me, the path to success was already laid. My father and mother were a very well respected and loved couple in the black community, both of my brothers were very good-looking and fearless when it came to sports and girls, and all my sisters were beautiful and very smart women. So I had no choice but to follow the mold, right?

Well, let's just say I definitely gave a different spin to the Mosely name and left my own personal signature on the community. I'm sorry, but when your last name is set so high on a pedestal, so connected to success and respectability and achievement, and you had nothing to do with it, it is plain to see that the only way for me to go with this situation was down.

Allow me to explain. I'm not making excuses because the bad decisions that I made were mine and mine alone.

But when you hear, "Oh you don't play football like your brother Steven did. He was so good," or "Your brother Dwight was very good at baseball—why aren't you?" or even "Your sister Deborah was so smart; she was one of my favorite students," or "Your sister Victoria never made any grade lower than an *A* all through high school," it makes it very difficult to find your own voice.

Because, hey, let's face it: a Mosely has already been there and done it and has a t-shirt to prove it.

I believe that there were two factors that gave me what I felt like was wiggle room to make bad decisions and somewhat get away with things that any of my siblings would not have gotten away with under any circumstance. First, the sibling nearest me in age was my sister Vanessa but she was five years older than I was, which gave ammunition for the other siblings to tease me about being adopted or that I was found in the garbage can and they took me in.

But that's a story for another day. What I mean to say is that my mother and father were a lot more relaxed with the rules with me than with my siblings. So they let me get away with a lot of things that the others probably did not. Secondly, we moved from the west side of town to a development called El Vista, or "the country" as we called it, where my father built a brand new home. This move took me away from my extended family, including the Johnsons, the Wilsons, the Cunninghams, all the families in the neighborhood and the people who'd had the responsibility to whip me and raise me when my mother and father were not around—my support system.

Since my brothers and sisters were off starting their lives and my mother was taking flower arrangement classes and Daddy was working all the time I seemed to have quite a bit of idle time and you know what they say, "The idle man is the playground for the devil," and he had a quite a time with me.

My oldest brother, Steven, was my only sibling who still lived in the city of Port Arthur while I was growing up. I used to spend a lot of time at his house with his wife, Angela, and their daughter, my niece Tanya. Angela used to take us everywhere with her and she was a lot of fun, especially when we visited her family. As I said earlier Angela was one of thirteen children in her family and at least four of them were close to my age, so it was always a ball hanging with them.

One particular day Angela took Tanya and me to Gibson's Department Store. Gibson's back then was what Wal-Mart is today. After walking around and checking everything out somehow I ended up in the music section of the store, and I began flipping through the 45's and found a few from my favorite artists: The Ohio Players, Cameo, Con Funk Shun, The Jackson Five, and Earth, Wind & Fire. I thought to myself that if I slipped a few of these 45's down my pants no one would see them and I could go home and really have fun with them. So I did. I shoved about four or five of those records down the front of my pants and began walking toward the exit. At that point no one stopped me or said anything to me so I thought if I could just make it to the car I would be home free.

So when I pushed open the heavy doors of the store and walked out I saw the car right up front and just as I was going to make a mad dash for it I felt someone's hand on my right shoulder and another hand patting my front zipper right where the 45's were and the two hands had a voice, and the voice said, "You want to come back in the store and talk about what's in your pants?"

If I had died right then you would have never known it because my heart was beating so fast it would not have allowed me to die. As I walked back through the store I did not see Angela or Tanya or anyone that I knew. That gave me relief because I did not want my father to know anything about this.

Huh, that's funny. Even today I realize that I was never afraid of my father for the punishment that came with my bad behavior but of the disappointment my bad behavior caused him. When security and the store manager finally got me in the back room I was a scared little rabbit, and when I saw the two-way glass I knew that I was dead. They were looking right at me the whole time. I'd thought I was slick and getting away with something but they had me cold dead to rights.

I wasn't even listening when the security guard was telling me that this kind of behavior was going to land me in prison if I kept it up, but I perked up and heard everything he said when he told me he was going to call my father down to pick me up. I jumped up and began begging the man.

"Please, I came here with my big sister. She will take me home." I thought if I could get Angela alone maybe I could convince her not to tell my brother and that way maybe it wouldn't get back to my daddy. But then the store manager butt in and told me he'd already seen Angela and told her to go home because only a parent could pick up a child from custody after any type shoplifting incident. Again, even if I wanted to die, my heart would not allow it because it was beating way too fast. Right then and there I fell to my knees, I clutched both hands together, and I looked into the eyes of the store manager and the security guards.

"Please, take me to jail. I promise I will stay there as long as you want me to, just please don't call my father."

The store manager repeated what I said to make sure he heard me right. "You mean to tell me that you would rather go to jail, for as long as I like, just as long as I did not call your father?"

"Yes, please."

He snickered and said, "Well don't that just beat all. Son, I'm sorry to tell you but we already called your father, and he's on his way here right now. He should be here in about five minutes." I just collapsed on the floor crying.

When my father arrived he passed a few words back and forth with the store manager. A slight smile curled from his lips as he walked toward me, and then I saw the all-too-familiar side-to-side shake of his head which I have always understood as the signal for his disappointment in my bad behavior.

The ride home was silent, not even music from Dad's AM radio.

The silence was momentarily broken by only one word from my father: "Why?"

Then silence again.

Then he asked, "Is there a reason your behavior is getting worse? Is it something your mother and I are doing that is making you act this way?"

Then silence again. I believe that people with addiction call it "a moment of clarity," but whatever it was that made this come out of me I believe it was the truest thing I have ever said in my life. It was as if I knew I was on the desert and needed a drink of water.

"Dad, I feel alone. I don't know anyone and it seems that no one knows me. Since we moved I don't feel connected to no one anymore. Everyone is so far away. I feel like no one cares about me or worries about me or wants to see me do well." For the first time I realized what my brothers and sisters had growing up that I had been taken away from early in life. My history.

Since we moved I had not seen my Aunt Rose; her sister, Aunt Franni; my Nanny Jane; Tyra; or Debra and their cousin Sarah—all who lived on my old block. I hadn't seen the Woods, the Johnsons, the Cunninghams, or my best good friend Mark Taylor who lived across the street. I realize that it may sound like an excuse to explain away my bad behavior but think about it like this.

As a kid when you went bowling they would put up those guards on both sides of the lane so that no matter how you threw the ball the ball would still stay in the lane and would eventually hit something. Well my neighborhood and all of its families were my side rails and all of a sudden they were not there to keep me "straight on the lane." It was getting hard for me to tell if I was heading to the gutter or not.

The car went silent again. Then my father pulled over and stopped the car. He shifted the car into park and then he raised his right hand and set it on my left shoulder and he spoke low, slow, and monotone.

He said, "Son, close your eyes."

I did.

Then he said, "You hear my voice, right?"

I said, "Yes."

He said, "Can you see me in your mind?"

"Yes, I can."

"Can you see your Aunt Rose and your aunt Franni?"

"Yes."

"What about your sisters, your brothers? Mark, Jason, Tyra and Debra, and Sarah?"

I said, "Yes."

Then he told me to open my eyes. And then he said this: "Son, whenever you are making a decision to do anything, whether it is something good or bad or just making a decision about life itself, close your eyes and hear my voice. Picture me and your sisters and brothers and the whole neighborhood that you came from. Understand and remember the sacrifices that others have made for you to get where you are and to help you to become the person that you are today. Just hear my voice and remember, Son, just hear my voice."

My father recognized that his lessons would always stay with me if I just stopped and thought first and remembered his words, if I just closed my eyes and heard his voice. My father is no longer here in the physical sense, but to this day I still hear his voice. He is my voice of reason. I cannot tell you that I never disappointed my father again, but I can tell you that because I could hear my father's voice— and I still can—I started to make better decisions.

Age Four, Contemplating
doing something wrong

Age Thirteen, Just Before I Got Caught

Chapter 6

Responsibility Is A Heavy Responsibility

$\mathfrak{M}$y mother used to say my father was a man before he was a man because of how he always handled his responsibilities even at a young age. My father was the baby of nine kids. There were five girls and four boys. After being promoted to the eleventh grade, my father quit high school and took a job as a seaman, which was a typical route for most black men at that time. It was either that or work at one of the many oil refineries that existed in our little town of Port Arthur, Texas.

While on the ship, my father recognized that being a seaman was not something that he wanted to do all his life, so he enrolled in a correspondence school to get his high school diploma. Can you imagine passing a test covering material that you were never taught and without having anyone to ask questions if you got confused? That is simply amazing!

There are three times in my life that I can say for certain that my father emphasized to me the importance of handling responsibility. I am sure there were many, many more but these three incidents stick out most vividly in my mind. It is certain that I failed him on at least two of these occasions—the third one we will talk about later.

The first time my father talked to me about being responsible was when he bought me a mini bike, and he made me promise on several occasions never to ride it in the street.

It was a very small mini bike, a Honda 50. Top speed was about 15 miles per hour downhill with the wind howling at my back. I remember disappointing my father the many times he rode past me in his car shaking his head side to side and then speeding off.

The second time was when he bought me my first car. He made me promise to keep up the maintenance on it so that it would last me a long time. To this day, I can still see my father shaking his head from side to side as he pulled up ready to tow the car home after the engine blew up from me not adding water to the car when the light came on. I had owned the car for approximately three months. Even today I feel his pain.

The joke was that every time my father came back to shore he left a baby. As to the findings, daddy must have come home at least seven times because in my particular family I am the baby of seven—four girls and three boys. Out of all the kids that were born to Walter and Jessie Mosely there were two things that were out of the ordinary: one, I was the only child that my father saw born. He was either going out to sea or coming in from the sea while the other six were being born. And two, I was blessed to take the name of my father, Walter Mosely, Jr. I had two older brothers and for some reason my older brother Steven did not get named after my father and neither did my other brother Dwight.

In hindsight I believe my mother and father may have wanted to rethink that decision, but I digress.

The responsibility of taking care of seven kids, a wife, and a home for a black man in the sixties should have been enough but out of all the other five girls and three other brothers in his family my father also took care of his mother until the day she died. She was a little over one hundred years old so that was a long time.

My father once told me that being young and free to make any choices without consequences was the most dangerous thing in the world. It is almost certain a wrong choice will be made unless you truly understand the responsibility of responsibility.

One cool evening in October when I was sixteen years old, my father walked in my room while I was making love to my girlfriend and scared the hell out of all three of us. After the initial shock, he closed the door to a crack and demanded that we put our clothes on, get off the bed, and wait for him to return. Although my girlfriend and I were scared out of our wits for getting caught, I believe we were more frightened of what my father was going to say or do when he came back. My father was a big man, about 6'1" in height and close to 235 pounds and very solid. That was real big for men back in the day. He had the biggest hands I have ever seen on a man in my life, and I had felt them on my behind more than once.

When my father finally came back (which felt like forever but truly was about maybe five minutes), he gave me and my girlfriend my third lesson in handling responsibility.

He said, "Son, I believe that what you and your girlfriend were doing was beautiful. There is nothing in the world more meaningful than sharing yourself with the one you love. It is the ultimate expression of what and how you feel, and I would not tell you not to do it if it is the expression that you must share with each other. Although you both are physically ready to handle this action, I can honestly tell you that neither of you are mature enough to handle this awesome responsibility of engaging in sexual intercourse."

He went on to tell us that if I had been ready for that responsibility, I would not have done it in someone else's home because the neighbors would think that my father condoned this type of behavior with him present. Secondly, he said I was not being responsible because this girl loved me enough to allow me to put her in that situation and that I had failed her as well. Then he explained to us that the responsibility we took to have fun came with the responsibility of safety, condoms, and birth control. He made me see that the responsibility to make a decision came with the responsibility of the outcome of that decision.

He ended with the notion that responsibility was a very heavy responsibility and that neither of us should tread on it lightly.

Oh, and the embarrassment of having to sit there with my girlfriend and listen to my father talk about the responsibilities of sex after he'd caught me in the act in his home, well, that was part of that lesson too…

My Fathers Business Key Ring for Advertising

Chapter 7

Mind Your

Front Row, Son

While growing up and spending much of that time with my father I realized that my father knew just about everybody in our little city and just about everybody knew him. If they did not know him by sight, they would surely know him by name. But I also realized that other than his brothers and maybe a handful of people around town, the circle of people that my father called his friends was very, very small. My father was very particular about whom he even called a friend and also whom he spent his time with or around. But it was quite the opposite for me. In fact, if you knew my name and I knew yours, lifelong friends we would instantly become. My motto was, the only reason you aren't my friend is because I haven't met you…yet.

Speaking of one of my friends, I had this one by the name of Wendell Jones. We used to get together after school and on weekends to roam the city in search of two things: some good pickup games of basketball and some hot girls. Honestly, we found more hot girls than basketball games usually. Anyway, Wendell was an inch or so taller than I was, brown-skinned, short neat haircut, and thick. He wasn't heavy, just big-boned, and he always had a serious expression on his face. If you didn't know him well he would come off a little mean or gruff, but he was a big softy. And when we were together all we did was laugh.

Wendell was always cleanly dressed and very soft-spoken, but he had a definite way with the girls. He used to call me his little brother when we went out to clubs and parties, and that made me feel pretty good. He would somewhat protect me from all the dudes that wanted to get at me for some reason or another and that only solidified what I felt was a true friendship between us two. Wendell had a rough upbringing; well, at least, that's how I saw it.

It was only he and his mother and a lot of different male figures in his life. Wendell had no car of his own and the piece of car his mother had seemed to always stop on her. I would see it broken down on the side of the road quite a bit during my comings and goings which is one reason why he and I hung out so much. He always needed a ride. On the weekends when we would go out, I never picked him up from his home. He would always walk to my house and end up completing his ensemble at my expense by wearing a jacket of mine that went well with his slacks or "Hey, that tie sure goes good with my shirt," and "By the way, you still got that cologne you wore the other night?" But hey, we were buddies, and we were going out together, and *you want your boy to be as fly as you, right?*

Wendell never had any money and the testimony came every time we went out to party. First off he never had five dollars to put on the gas; I would always pay for him to get into whatever party or club we went to; and on the way home when we were hungry he never had a couple of bucks to get himself something to eat at three o'clock in the morning at Jack –in- the- Box. But hey, that's my friend; we were together. I had the money, and he said he would get me the next time. Well, one night Wendell showed me just how good a friend he was and my lesson of "mind your front row" began.

My father was a member of this professional society called the Royalist Social and Civic Club. It was a society of like-minded professional black leaders that had made great strides in their chosen professions and who had given back tremendously to the black community as a whole. It was quite an elite and powerful group of men. There was Mr. Moody Harris who owned the city's funeral home, Mr. I.Z. Machenry (my father's mentor) who owned his own life insurance agency, Mr. Jonah Davis (a fellow seaman) who owned a couple of general stores, and many more very important men in the city. Often they gave parties that they called "balls" which usually kept my mother and father out till around midnight or a little after.

Well, on one of those ball nights Wendell had planned for us to meet up with Shari Francis and Maxine Green, two adopted sisters whose parents were out of town. I asked my father if I could use my mother's car to go chase some girls with Wendell, but because I hadn't cut the grass or done some menial chores that day, my father forbid me to use my mother's car. He also added, "You need to mind your front row with that one."

Because my father knew that I was prone to mischief, for good measure he thought ahead and keep me honest by taking the entire set of keys with him when he and my mother left to go to the Royalist Club's social event that evening. Well, I must say that my father was right about one thing and totally wrong about another.

He was correct that I was prone to mischief, but he was dead wrong for thinking that he would keep me honest by thinking ahead of me and taking the set of keys with him because I had already thought ahead of *him* and taken only the car's ignition key off the ring. I just sat back and waited for my mother and father to leave the house so that my evening could get started as Wendell and I had planned.

The second that my father's little blue Dodge Dart took that left turn on H.O. Mills' Boulevard, I called Wendell and told him to high-tail it on over to the house because the party was on and popping.

On our way to Shari and Maxine's house, I informed Wendell of the situation with the key and the key ring and that my mother and father usually got home by midnight or half past at the latest. I also informed him of the peril that would be awaiting me if for some ungodly reason I did not get that big brown Plymouth Gran Sedan back in the garage by eleven-thirty that night. He agreed and we continued on our quest.

At Shari and Maxine's we sat on the couch hugging, kissing, and doing what teenagers do when Wendell pulled me aside and said, "Divide and conquer." That was the code that meant if we separated the girls more would probably happen for each of us. I agreed, but what Wendell said next sent a slow chill up my spine.

He said, "Give me the keys to the car and I will take Maxine around the corner so you can make your move on Shari." Now, surely Wendell had been right there in the car with me when I told him about the sensitive timing situation. I remember looking into his face because he was my boy, I knew he would not let me down like that. Oh no, not my main man Wendell. I had paid for too many nights to go into the clubs. I had lost so many jackets and ties that I never got back from him because I forgot to make him take my clothes off when we returned from partying. I had fed this friend of mine too many late-night tacos and burgers for him to let me down in that simple way.

So what do I say, but, "Okay, it's cool. But remember, we are on the clock."

He said, and I remember his words as clear as if he said them to me today: "Don't worry. I got you."

To this day I still do not believe anyone at any time when those words are spoken anywhere around or to me. Ten-thirty came. Then eleven. Eleven-thirty came. Then midnight. Twelve-thirty came and went with no sign of Wendell. Finally, at

12:55 Wendell pulls up smiling saying, "You get some?"

In one fluid motion, I punched the shit out of Wendell Jones, took the keys out of his hands before he hit the ground, and ran for the car. As I turned the corner on two wheels, leaving marks on the road from Shari and Maxine's house, I hear Wendell yelling in the background.

"You coming back for me? Okay, I'll just wait here then." After cussing Wendell out in every possible language known to man including Hebrew, I began praying a very detailed and specific prayer because I wanted God to get this one exactly right:

"Father, when I get home and raise that garage door, Lord, please do not let that 1972 blue Dodge Dart Swinger with the scratch on the passenger-side door right underneath the door handle be in that garage on 601 47th Street, Port Arthur, Texas 77640." If I'd known those extra four numbers of the zip code, I would have prayed them too.

But my prayers were not answered: Mother and Father were home! Hell, I guess I needed those last four digits of that damn zip code.

As I stood there frozen with my right arm raised in the air from opening the garage door and the shock of seeing my father's car in that garage, I'm sure I looked just like the statue of liberty. All I could think to myself was, "Do I have enough gas to make it to Mexico?" Knowing that I didn't, I figured, "Well, I can only be killed once, so let's face the music."

I eased through the back door which led to the kitchen. Then I slid passed the couch and television that was in the den. From there, I cruised down that long hallway that immediately smelled like Pine-Sol because my grandmother's room was the first room on the left. There was no sound all the way to my room on the right which was directly across from the hall bathroom. Once in my room, I stood quiet for a moment to listen. There was no noise, no movement or sound coming from my mother and father's room. So I eased my clothes off, got under the covers, and felt pretty safe and snug. "They must be sleep, so I guess I'll hear about it in the morning," I thought.

BLAM!! The door slams open. "Get yo ass up out that bed," my father screams.

"Dad, Dad, wait I can explain."

"Now you grown you can do anything you want in this house, right?" WHACK, WHACK with the belt.

I can still hear my mother's voice in the distance "Walter, don't kill my baby." That was the worst and last whipping I ever received from my father. As usual after my punishment my father and I had a calm talk.

He said: "Son, whenever I tell you to 'mind your front row' that's when I see you giving too much attention to the wrong people in your life. You have to think of your life as a stage, and the people you sit in the front row of your life will get the best part of you. These people should be your immediate family, relatives, and very, very close friends. If you find that any of these people take your best gifts, like your generosity, your patience, your kindness and trust, and they do not give any of their best gifts to you in return, then those people should be in the back row or even in the balcony of your life. Because they are farther away you are not so affected by them not giving back."

As we hugged and said goodnight, he told me to get some sleep because bright and early I was

71

going to cut that yard, the weeds, and anything else he could think of.

Once he left I could barely hear him talking to my mother. He said, "Damn, that boy is smart. You know it wasn't that he disobeyed me. I just can't believe he thought ahead of me to take the key off the ring. Uh, uh, uh, Jessie, we got to watch that boy."

NOTES

This park was built to honor My Father

Chapter 8

All Money Ain't GOOD MONEY

$\mathcal{U}$p until I was eight years old I had no idea that money could actually be good or bad. I didn't realize it had a choice. I did not know that it made a difference where money came from and that what was done with it could be construed as a bad thing. The little money I got from time to time was spent mostly on junk like candy and gum but after this lesson from my father I never looked at money quite the same ever again.

Earlier you read how my father took on and won a battle with City Hall for illegally Gerrymandering the voting districts to dilute the black vote. Well that accomplishment was only a drop in the ocean compared to the giants he took on when I was six years old.

The late sixties and early seventies seemed to be booming times for black Americans—at least that's how it looked to me from my young perspective. Especially in my city and my side of town—"the west side" —which was considered to be any area west of Houston Avenue. This area was then and still is to this day totally inhabited by black people. The two industries that kept our city thriving at that time were the ports where cargo would go out and come in from all over the world and the oil refineries which took crude oil and refined it for uses like making gasoline and plastic.

The three cities of Beaumont, Port Arthur, and Orange, Texas, were called the Golden Triangle because we were the proud owners of three major oil refineries right in our backyard. There was the Gulf, Texaco, and Fina refineries. Although both of these industries only gave out menial jobs back then to the black man they paid well enough to take care of and keep the black family together.

At a very young age—the tenth grade—my father chose the port and the life of a seaman. He was young and adventurous, and life on the sea came with travel and wonder. Also it gave seamen the opportunity to make as much money as they wanted. If you needed more money, you could go on more trips. If you needed a break you just did not go on any trips.

The refinery jobs gave a set amount of money per hour labored. I asked my father once why he never worked for any of the refineries. And he would answer, "I don't like someone telling me what I'm worth per hour." I understood that quite well, because my father had a free spirit. He was a thinker a mover and a shaker, so to speak. Later I would come to find that the apple did not fall from the tree. And for what he needed at the time — money to feed a family of seven and his mother— being a seaman fulfilled his needs.

Eventually my father left the sea and became self-employed. As I said earlier the city was thriving off of the two industries that were available to the people of Port Arthur. And from these two industries other services needed to be met.

Black families were growing and neighborhoods were expanding. People needed cars, houses, gasoline, clothes, appliances, and an array of goods and services. My father saw the need and answered the call and became a licensed real estate and independent insurance agent. He also became involved in quite a few community boards and committees, some that significantly changed the life of all the people of the city of Port Arthur and that make a difference even to this very day.

Because black people were making more money, black people began to venture out and do more things. Black entrepreneurs began starting their own businesses to make sure that the money stayed in the black community. Businesses like full-service gas stations, flower shops, car lot owners, plumbers, electricians, painters, new appliance stores, men and women's clothiers, shoe stores, and, of course, real estate and independent life insurance agents.

Because of this massive growth my father noticed the property taxes began to inflate to an enormous rate—so much so that he got himself appointed to and chaired a three-member equalization board whose purpose was to provide a time and place for private tax payers to appeal the appraisal values of their properties.

What my father also noticed was that the refineries were making an obscene amount of money each year but were paying less in taxes than some homeowners. He vowed it would change.

Around this same time my father used to take me back and forth to the old neighborhood so I could visit my best good friend Mark Taylor. I had a little mini bike that my dad would pack in the trunk of the car so that Mark and I could have a high old time while I was there visiting. But there was this one guy named Kenneth Frazier who was a little older than we were but for some reason or another he would always hang around us younger kids. He often got into trouble and would drag some of the other young kids into trouble with him. He would always entice us to come along with him by offering us money.

He would say, "I'll give you fifty cents if you jump Mrs. Allan's fence and steal five of her plums." Or, "I bet you a dime you can't throw a rock and bust that street light out." Now, true enough, most of the time we would do it for ourselves for free but, hey, if Kenneth Frazier was offering fifty cents for the same plums we got for free and ten cents for a broken street light we were more than likely going to try to break it anyway, hey, let's do this.

Lincoln High School was right across the street from our house on 1048 Roosevelt. It was quite often that my best good friend Mark and I and the rest of the gang would play either on the baseball or football field of the campus or if we found a stray tennis ball we would play almost all day on the tennis court. But one day old Kenneth Frazier found us playing in the back of the boys' gym parking lot and he said he had a quarter for every window we busted out. Listen, there were not enough rocks…

Riding in the car with my father on the way home from a meeting I noticed my father was rather irritated. The meeting had been unusual because of where the meeting had been held and who the meeting was with. The meeting was at a restaurant in Beaumont, a little city about nine miles away from Port Arthur, and it was with two men in suits with briefcases. Being that my father was a real estate and insurance agent he was usually the one with the briefcase, and we usually met the customers at the house they were buying or at their home to discuss insurance, and the customers never wore suits. To top it all off, my father had left his briefcase in the car sitting next to me.

After much silence in the car between us, my father asked me if I knew what a bribe was.

I answered, "Isn't that the person who marries the groom?"

He laughed and said, "No son, a bribe is when someone offers you money to do something that you would not normally do, something out of your character, something wrong to benefit them."

"Is that what those men wanted with you?"

He said yes, and I asked if it was a lot of money.

He said, "More money than I would make in a lifetime."

"Wow." After thinking about this a little bit I asked my father, "Will anyone get hurt or go to the hospital for what they are giving you money to do?"

He looked at me curiously and said, "No, not physically hurt, but hurt in many other ways."

So I asked, "What do they want you to do, Daddy?"

He began telling me how this three-member board that he chaired was getting ready to hire an independent appraisal auditor to reassess the property values and include the refineries so that they would pay their fair share of property taxes and ease the burden on homeowners. He also told me that the refinery people had already gotten to the mayor, a few city councilmen, and one of the members of my father's three-member board, but they would not say which one. He said that they only needed him to vote yes to keep the current tax structure and not to ask for the independent tax appraisal, and the money was his.

I asked my father if he saw the money.

And he said, "Yes."

I asked, "They were going to let you take it right then?"

"Yes," he said. "Son, remember this. All money is not good money. The money that these companies will be paying in taxes will go to pay for uniforms for your school's football and basketball teams. It will build bridges and roads for us to get around on in this city. The money will save homeowners hundreds if not thousands of dollars so that your friends and our neighbors can send their kids to college or save for rainy days. That's what good money does.

"When money is given to do bad things or to compromise your own moral character then that is bad money, Son. All money ain't good money." Then there was silence on the ride all the way home.

Back at the boy's gym with Kenneth Frazier, I was up to a dollar and twenty-five cents for the five broken windows I had broken out. Mark was the only one that was closest to me with three windows broke. Right at that time Mr. Meyers the drama teacher drove up in the parking lot and caught us breaking the window out of the boy's gymnasium.

As we began to run like bats out of hell I was unfortunately recognized and called out by name.

Mr. Meyers recognized me from when my father and I would pick up my sister Vickie who was in his drama class and from a few late afternoon rehearsals for some plays she was in.

The first thing he said was, "You know your parents taught you better than that," and he was right they did. Quietly sitting in the back of Mr. Meyers' car as he drove Mark and me home, we listened to him scold us about our behavior and told us how much we hurt the school and how this would affect the game that was to be played that night.

I hadn't realized how many people we had hurt with our money-making bad behavior, but it hit me square in the face when I saw my father standing on the porch shaking his head side to side in total disappointment.

After the good whipping I got from my dad he asked, "What on God's green earth would make you want to bust out windows at the school?"

I explained to him about Kenneth Frazier and the twenty-five cents per window.

He reiterated the lesson and said, "That is exactly what we talked about the other night, Son. That's bad money. You were paid to compromise your character to do something you knew was wrong. You will have to find a way to make this up, Son—not to me, but to yourself."

The next day I went to the school and apologized to Coach Grable, the head basketball coach at the school, and I gave him my one dollar and twenty-five cents. For the next couple of weeks I swept out the gymnasium as a way to work off the money to repair the rest of the windows. Of course my father worked that part out. But no amount of money in the world could have made me feel better than when my father said he was proud of me for doing that. Character Restored.

By the way, the tax situation broke down like this. The taxes for the people of Port Arthur started out at $1.78 per $100.00 of appraised property value and the refineries were paying only $685,000 a year. After my father cast the deciding vote the citizens of Port Arthur paid only $.73 per $100.00 of appraised property value, and each refinery was paying over eight million dollars a year—which is still the model that is used today.

NOTES

Walter Mosely, Sr., 1977

Chapter 9

Check Your Lost and Found

While growing up in the 1970s in a little town called Port Arthur, Texas, there were, oddly enough, quite a few things to get into, and, believe me, I found my fair share. But one thing that occupied my mind to the fullest was spending time with my dad because every day was an adventure with him. You see, while other dads were leaving their homes in the morning and going to their factory and oil refining jobs which allow only two fifteen-minute breaks and a half-hour off for lunch taken right there at the job, my father was going places and doing things all over the city. In fact, it was said, if you sat in one spot of the city long enough, you would probably see my father's little blue 1972 Dodge Dart pass by two or three times in a day.

He would go to the bank, to the appraisal office, to a mortgage company, show a house, go to an appointment to talk to some people about insurance, show another house, go to a closing, and I wanted to be right there with him because I did not want to miss a thing. He just fascinated me with all the people he knew and who knew him and all the knowledge that he possessed. Every time he got out of the car he would be stopped by two or three people either going in or coming out of the place he was going to do some business, and they would start talking about any and everything.

It seemed like no matter what I or anyone else asked my father, he knew the answer and could explain in detail how, when, where, and who was involved when it happened. Now I know where I got my long-windedness from.

As the years went by and because of all the time I'd spent with my father, it seemed to me that my father had developed a sixth sense about me. Some kind of way, he could always tell when I had lost my identity or when I was trying to find myself among other people. You see, because I hung around my father so much, I never had a chance to get into the bad things that life had to offer. Oh, don't get me wrong; I was very mischievous, and believe me, I found my way into trouble pretty easy and often. Just ask any of my siblings or my siblings' friends. But the real trappings, the ones that can consume or ruin your life like drugs, gambling, and alcohol—those are the ones that did not have an opportunity to enter my life.

My father himself was not a drinker, so to say. Socially he would "take a little taste" as he called it just for the company of others that he kept. But to go to a bar or even drink a beer in the house alone was a sight I had never seen. So, consequently, I did not drink either. In fact to this day I have never smoked a cigarette or inhaled marijuana. Hell, I did not have a drink of beer until my first year of college.

That was exactly when I started hearing my father's voice in the back of my mind saying these exact words: "Check your lost and found." You see, in my high school days I was a bit of a jock. I played basketball for the Thomas Jefferson Fighting Yellow Jackets. I was a power forward. One weekend when my mother and father were on a city councilman business trip, I had the fellas over to the house for some "cutting up."

At one point during the cutting up, one of my teammates pulled out a joint, lit it up, and began smoking it. Then he began to pass it around to the other fellas. Each of the guys had their own way of smoking the joint which told me they had done this before. One or two of my teammates would take the joint and inhale the smoke deeply then wave the joint under their noses in a circle and breathe in more that way. Some would take short quick hits on the joint, and then hold their heads up and pinch their nose off like if they did not the smoke would fall out of their heads.

Then the joint was passed to me. As I took hold of the joint, I could literally hear my father's voice telling me to "check it, check it, check your lost and found" which was what my father would tell me whenever he found me searching for myself, being a follower and not a leader, losing myself to someone else's ways and needing to find my way back to his original instructions.

But what was I to do? It was clear that my teammates had indulged in this type of behavior before and were old hands at it; but to me, this was something new, something I had never done before, something I knew that my father would not approve of. Although I was comfortable with the person that I was, I was still trying to gain acceptance and fit in with the group—which was no easy task. If I pushed it away, I could be ridiculed, talked about, laughed at. They would call me a square, a punk, or push me out of the group altogether.

But on the other hand, if I did it and became one of them I would betray my father's trust and not stand up to the things I was raised to believe were wrong or not right for me. What was I to do? As the moment got more uncomfortable for me and everyone in the room, I noticed that it felt like everything was going in slow motion.

I raised the joint up to my mouth, sucked in on the twisted white stalk, and as my mouth began to fill with this smoke, I realized that I did not know what to do with it. I did not know if I was supposed to swallow the smoke like a mouthful of water or breathe it in like a breath of oxygen, so I just held it in my jaws. I just held the smoke right there in my jaws looking like Dizzy Gillespie mid-note with the joint still in my hand until someone said, "Damn Bo, don't hog the joint, man, give it up."

I gladly and quickly passed it on to the next guy with no one ever noticing that I just blew the smoke out of my mouth without actually inhaling it. Later when the guys were laid out and fumbling around from being high, I just pretended to do the same so I would not stand out or draw attention to myself. I wanted them to think that I was one of them that I smoked and got high from the weed, too.

When my father finally returned from his trip, I told him what had happened. He asked me how I felt about the whole event. I told him I felt like I had let him down because I'd clearly disobeyed him by doing something I knew was not right. But I also felt weak and cheap and angry at myself that I would act like I was high in front of others to gain their acceptance or feel worthy to be around them.

My father put his hand on my shoulder and said, "It is not necessary to rely on others for your happiness or self-worth. You will have to learn to accept who you are completely, the good and the bad. And, you should only make changes to yourself as YOU see fit, not because you think someone else wants you to, but because you know that your future will be better for it. My father then took his very large right hand and placed it over my heart and said, "Listen to me, Son, inside of you is a big box labeled 'lost and found' and in this box are all the lessons and conversations that we have had over the years.

"Now in those times that you find yourself searching or looking for an answer to any of these problems or situations that life throws at you, just check your lost and found and the answers will come. Just reach down deep and search in that box and find the values and the principles that your mother and I have taught you and I'm sure you will be just fine." After I stood up, hugged my father, and began to walk away I was feeling pretty good that I had enough information and back-up from my father to fight anything that came my way.

Then my father said, "Oh yeah, hold on a minute, Son." As I turned to see what my father wanted I noticed him taking off his belt.

I said, "Dad, what's up?"

"I'm glad you learned your lesson, Son, and I truly feel that you will never do this again but don't get me wrong. You smoked weed in my house and for that I'm gone have to whip that ass." And so the story goes...

Walter Mosely

High School Graduation Picture 1980

Chapter 10

Remember To

Stay In Your Lane

$\mathcal{H}$ave you ever noticed that every church has this one deacon who always stays late and counts the church offering, makes out the deposit slips, and then has the responsibility to go to the bank and deposit the money? That was my father, which, needless to say, just gave me another reason not to want to attend church. My mother did not like it either.

When Daddy would finally come walking up to the car Momma would always say, "Here comes your daddy. His t-hind is slow as Moses," which was news to me because I never read in all my bible classes that Moses was ever known to be slow, but I was only eight years old so maybe I hadn't read that far yet. There were two reasons, though, and two reasons only why I did enjoy going to church. Neither reason had anything to do with actually being in church but where we went and what happened after church.

Every Sunday after church we went out to eat, sometimes at The Bonanza Steakhouse on Gulf Way Drive or at my favorite place The Brisket Room over on Twin City Highway. The food at both places was simply amazing and the service that we received at each restaurant made us feel like rock stars.

It may have had something to do with the fact that my father had helped the owner of the Bonanza Steak House appeal the appraisal value of his home which ended up saving him thousands of dollars a year in property taxes. And that my father had sold the owner of The Brisket Room their new home and had finagled some kind of really good deal for him. Neither of those businessmen would ever let my father forget the good deals he'd made for them. We always received something extra on our plates, a free dessert, or one of our meals wouldn't made it on the bill if we received a bill at all. I wanted to eat there everyday since most of the time the food was free.

But my father would tell me, "You always want to be a welcomed surprise, not surprised that you are welcomed." I didn't know what that meant but I'm sure it meant we would not be eating their everyday. The second reason I liked Sundays after church was because my father would allow me to drive all the way back home.

I used to enjoy waving at all my friends and neighbors as we passed by and of course my father would allow me to blow the horn to make sure they would all wave back. This would pretty much annoy my mother to no end. She would comment on everything that I did wrong and would end each comment with a mumbled, "He's gonna kill us all just watch." But I paid her no mind because that was the highlight of my week. Because I could not reach the pedals, my father would handle the accelerator and the brake; my job was to sit on his lap, steer, and just keep the car inside the white or yellow striped lines.

Anytime I veered off the path or was heading for another lane or the shoulder, my father would say in a calm protective voice, "Stay in your lane, Son, stay in your lane." I would hear my mother's voice also but, believe me, you don't want to know what she was saying. As I got older and, of course, started to drive more and more, I did not need my father to work the pedals anymore. In fact, sometimes after he'd had a long day at work, I would drive my father home and allow him to be the passenger. During our conversation on the way home every now and then I would lose focus, and I would begin to drift into another lane and my father would look up and say, "Stay in your lane, Son, stay in your lane."

I would say, "Sorry, Dad," correct myself, and we would make it home safe and sound.

In August of 1980 I was poised to attend my first year of college. My father and I made the long drive to Wiley College in Marshall, Texas, together. He wanted to make sure he had that last little bit of time with his boy before he left me to become a man—at least that's what he said. Because there was no such thing as a GPS system in those days, we used a good old-fashioned road map to navigate a few back roads to get there. At one point, we stopped at a little gas station to switch drivers, use the restroom, get some gas, and to check the map to make sure we were going in the right direction.

As par for the course, on this five-and-half to six-hour drive my father took the opportunity to use the time and the map to give me another life lesson.

With one foot on the bumper, one hand palm-down on the fender, and the map sprawled out on the hood of the car, my father asked me to show him our starting point on the map. I pointed out the words *Port Arthur* which my father had circled in red with a magic marker the night before. He then asked me to point to our destination, and I pointed to the word *Marshall* which my father had circled in green.

He then said, "Do you see all the roads we could have taken to get to our destination?"

I answered, "Yes, Dad, I see them."

"Do you know why we chose the road we are on?"

I replied, "Yeah, because the other roads would have taken longer and we have never been down those roads before and we don't know exactly where they go to."

He said, "That is correct." Then he put his hand on my shoulder and said, "Son, we all take different roads sometimes to get to the same location and that's okay. What I want you to be aware of is not to get caught up in someone else's lane.

"What I am saying to you, Son, is that you are going to meet all kinds of people from all over the world here in college. And each and every one of them has his own road or lane he used in life to get here.

"In order for you to maintain your course, it will be necessary for you to always stay in your lane for your own personal journey. The fast lane of drugs and alcohol is not what you have been taught. The slow lane of laziness and irresponsibility is not what got you to this point in your life. The road and the lane you took to get here were laid out by me, your mother, and all your sisters and brothers. It was a long, rough, and hard lane you took but it was your lane. And the good thing about knowing your lane is that if you ever get lost you can take this same lane back to remind yourself who you are and where you come from; you can always get back to the person this family raised. Remember, Son, 'Just stay in your lane. Stay in your lane.'"

While I was in college my father wrote and called me quite often, and every letter and phone call that I got from him would end with the same phrase followed by, "Remember, I love you!"

NOTES

ABOUT THE AUTHOR

Walter Mosely, Jr., was born the baby and seventh child (four girls and three boys) of Walter and Jessie Mosely. He first recognized his aptitude for writing while attending Thomas Edison Junior High School. While there he was part of a journalism class that was responsible for getting out the weekly school newspaper. Walter had his own page in the paper called *Walter's Corner* where he was given free range to write poetry, news, and events as he saw fit for the school to read. He then attended and graduated from Thomas Jefferson High School where he played basketball and sang in the school's a cappella choir. From there he attended Wiley College in Marshall, Texas, where he spoke to the masses once again but this time on a much larger scale as one of the college and city's hottest DJ.

DJ Baby Love is a nickname that sticks to him to this day. Although this is Walter's very first attempt at writing, he is currently working on his next offering which will be the second in his series of three memoirs based on Knowledge: Father to Son Lessons. He also has his eyes on two fiction projects to be published in 2012 and 2013. We look forward to all that this exciting new author offers, and no matter what he writes, his style is one that surely delivers.

Walter Mosely, Jr.

And Even More Pictures!!

Vanessa   Me   Victoria

My Sisters and I Before Church.

"The Long Horn Ride"

1966 State Fair

Dwight   Me   Steven

After Church
with my Brothers

My Fathers City Councilman
Identification

During his 3rd Term

My Father 1967 in the

Old Neighborhood

My Dad and me

Walter Mosely, Sr.
&
Walter Mosely, Jr.

NOTES

Walter Mosely, Jr.

NOTES